HOW TO USE THIS BOOK

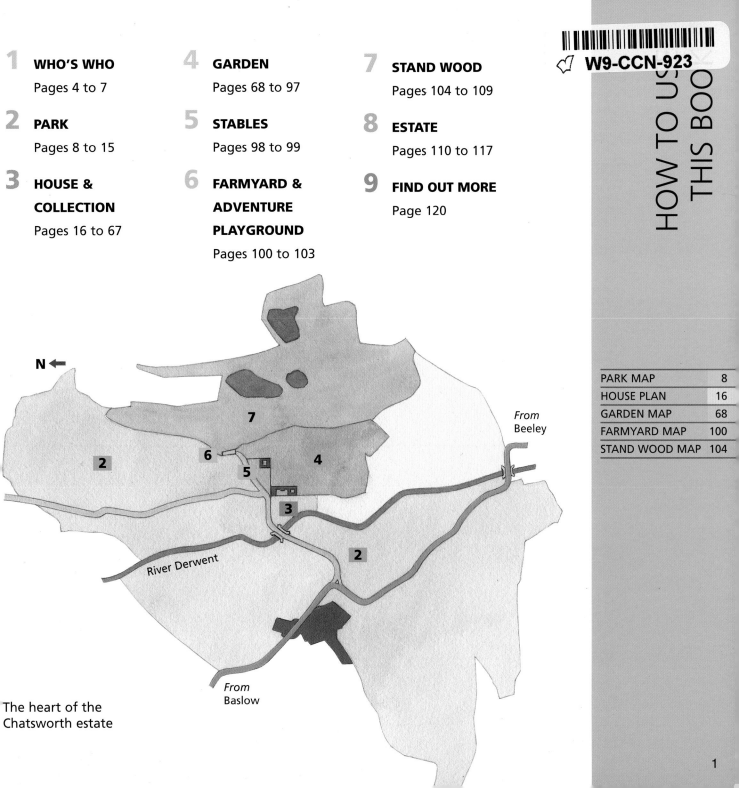

N ←

From Beeley

From Baslow

River Derwent

The heart of the Chatsworth estate

For five centuries, members of my family have welcomed guests from around the world. You are following in the footsteps of Queen Victoria, an entire school of wartime evacuees and actors such as Sir Anthony Hopkins and Keira Knightley on location, to name but a few.

As you will discover, each generation has made its own changes at Chatsworth; some I find inspiring, some bewildering, but all of them intriguing. Every visitor has a different view, which is what brings the place to life. On this page my wife and I have chosen some of the things that most fascinate us about Chatsworth. We hope you will enjoy finding your own favourite things with the help of this book.

Stoker Devonshire

Amanda Devonshire.

The Duke and Duchess of Devonshire

SCULPTURE

We share a passion for collecting contemporary sculpture, and the contrast between the modern forms and materials and this historic space is one we enjoy. One of our favourites is Allen Jones's Carefree Man, who tips his hat to welcome visitors on the Great Stairs Landing (page 34). In 2009 Allen made another sculpture for the garden, Déjeuner sur l'Herbe (page 98), a good place for a picnic.

SEASONS

The landscape is constantly changing and there is always something new to see. Look out for the bluebells and daffodils in the Pinetum (page 88) in spring time, tree peonies outside the 1st Duke's Greenhouse (page 74) in the summer and production at its peak in the Kitchen Garden (page 92) in August and September. In autumn the whole valley is filled with colour, and spectacular new views from the house and garden are revealed in winter, when the deciduous trees shed their leaves.

INNOVATION

The 6th Duke's Emperor Fountain (page 84) is powered not by pumps, but by the pressure of the water falling from a man-made moorland lake (page 70). It was the highest fountain of this kind in the world when it was built, and is one of many examples of exciting new ideas being tried out at Chatsworth. We work with the Chatsworth House Trust to continue this tradition of innovation and ensure that Chatsworth's history does not reach a full stop in the 21st century.

MATERIALS

Throughout the house there are window sills made from crinoidal limestone (above), a local stone which contains fossilised sea creatures. The views through the windows of the surrounding landscape are a reminder that the house is made from natural materials – stone, wood, glass and lead – many of which are drawn from the estate itself. It is the support of visitors and the efforts of staff that enables us to repair them when necessary.

PEOPLE

Most of all, Chatsworth would be nothing without the people – visitors and staff – who bring the place to life. The estate has an impressive tradition of long-service (some of those who recently received long-service awards, whether 10, 25, 40 or 50 years, are pictured above). If you have any questions at all while you are here, please do ask a member of staff, and if you see us about the place, please say hello.

Thank you for visiting.

BESS OF HARDWICK
1527-1608

m. (1) Robert Barlow
m. (2) Sir William Cavendish 1505-57
m. (3) William St. Loe
m. (4) George Talbot, 6th Earl of Shrewsbury

Bess married four times and rose from the gentry to the highest aristocracy. She and Sir William built Chatsworth with the money he made in the service of King Henry VIII.

1st Earl of Devonshire
William Cavendish
1552-1625

m. Anne Keighley
d.1625

Bess's second son was granted an Earldom. As there was already an Earl of Derby, he was given a vacant title, Devonshire.

2nd Earl of Devonshire
William Cavendish
1590-1628

m. Hon. Christian Bruce
1595-1675

Christian rebuilt the family fortune after the extravagant Earl's death.

3rd Earl of Devonshire
William Cavendish
1617-84

m. Lady Elizabeth Cecil
1619-89

The Cavendish family supported King Charles I in the English Civil War. After the King's defeat, the 3rd Earl narrowly avoided losing Chatsworth to Parliament.

4th Earl and 1ST DUKE of Devonshire
William Cavendish
1640-1707

m. Lady Mary Butler
1646-1710

The 4th Earl rebuilt Chatsworth as a **Baroque** palace, a statement of his power and ambition. He helped bring King William III and Queen Mary II to the throne. They awarded him the Dukedom in 1694.

2ND DUKE
of Devonshire

William Cavendish
1673-1729

m. Hon. Rachel Russell
1674-1725

The Duke was an active politician and the family's first serious collector of paintings, drawings, gems and coins.

3RD DUKE
of Devonshire

William Cavendish
1698-1755

m. Katherine Hoskins
d.1777

Following a disastrous fire in 1733, the Duke rebuilt his London home, Devonshire House in the new **Palladian** style promoted by the architect Richard Boyle, 3rd Earl of Burlington (1694/5-1753). The Duke's son married the Earl's daughter and heiress.

4TH DUKE
of Devonshire

William Cavendish
1720-64

m. Lady Charlotte Boyle
1731-54

Charlotte's inheritance brought the Cavendishes greater wealth and immense collections of fine art. The Duke was briefly Prime Minister. He hired 'Capability' Brown to improve the landscape park and James Paine to build the bridge and stables at Chatsworth.

CHATSWORTH HAS BEEN HANDED DOWN THROUGH 16 GENERATIONS OF THE CAVENDISH FAMILY, FROM FATHER TO ELDEST SON, OR THE NEAREST MALE HEIR.

5TH DUKE of Devonshire

William Cavendish
1748-1811

m. (1) Lady Georgiana
Spencer 1757-1806
m. (2) Lady Elizabeth
Foster 1757-1824

Devonshire House became the centre of **Whig** party politics and Georgiana reigned as queen of society and fashion. For two decades she and the Duke lived in a ménage-à-trois with Elizabeth Foster, who married the Duke after Georgiana's death.

6TH DUKE of Devonshire

William Spencer
Cavendish 1790-1858

The 'Bachelor Duke' modernised Chatsworth and built a new wing for his collections of books, minerals and contemporary sculpture. His Head Gardener, Joseph Paxton, re-designed and enlarged the garden.

7TH DUKE of Devonshire

William Cavendish
1808-91

m. Lady Blanche Howard
1812-40

After the extravagances of the 6th Duke, his second cousin, the 7th Duke, struggled to restore the family fortunes. His own investments, including development in Barrow-in-Furness, eventually caused greater debts.

8TH DUKE of Devonshire

Spencer Compton
Cavendish
1833-1908

m. Louise von Alten
1832-1911

The Duke refused three invitations from Queen Victoria to become Prime Minister. The new inheritance tax forced him to make major sales of the family's land, especially in Ireland.

9TH DUKE of Devonshire

Victor Cavendish
1868-1938

m. Lady Evelyn
Fitzmaurice 1870-1960

The nephew of the childless 8th Duke improved Chatsworth and was Governor-General of Canada from 1916 to 1921. He sold Devonshire House and Chiswick House in London at a time when many aristocratic London houses were being sold.

10TH DUKE of Devonshire

Edward Cavendish
1895-1950

m. Lady Mary Cecil
1895-1988

The Duke invited a girls' boarding school to use Chatsworth during the Second World War. His eldest son, William (1917-44), was killed in action. William's wife Kathleen Kennedy (1920-48), the sister of President John F Kennedy, died in an aeroplane accident.

11TH DUKE of Devonshire

Andrew Cavendish
1920-2004

m. Hon. Deborah Mitford
b.1920

After inheriting with 80% tax on all his land and possessions, the Duke created the Chatsworth House Trust to protect Chatsworth and its collections for future generations of visitors.

12TH DUKE of Devonshire

Peregrine Cavendish
b.1944

m. Amanda
Heywood-Lonsdale
b.1944

The present Duke and Duchess look after Chatsworth with the Chatsworth House Trust and pay rent to live in the house. Their Masterplan is restoring and enhancing Chatsworth for the future. They have three children and ten grandchildren.

WELCOME TO THE PARK

The park is open to walkers throughout the year.

1

Jubilee rock

2

Ice house

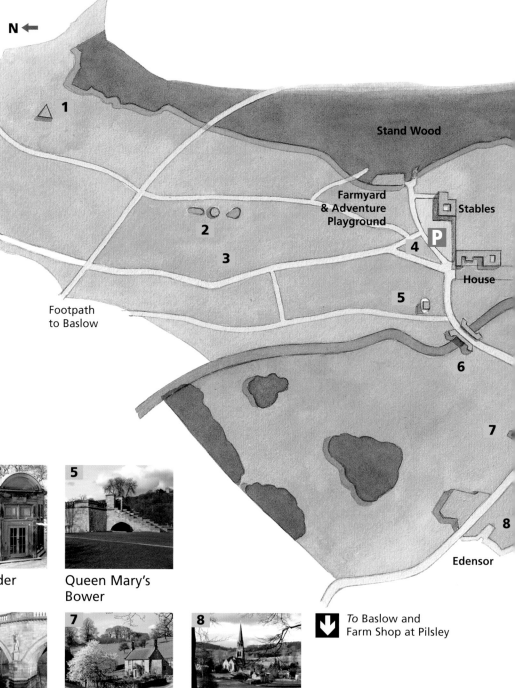

3

Sculptures

4

Game larder

5

Queen Mary's Bower

6

Paine's Bridge

7

Park Cottage

8

Edensor village

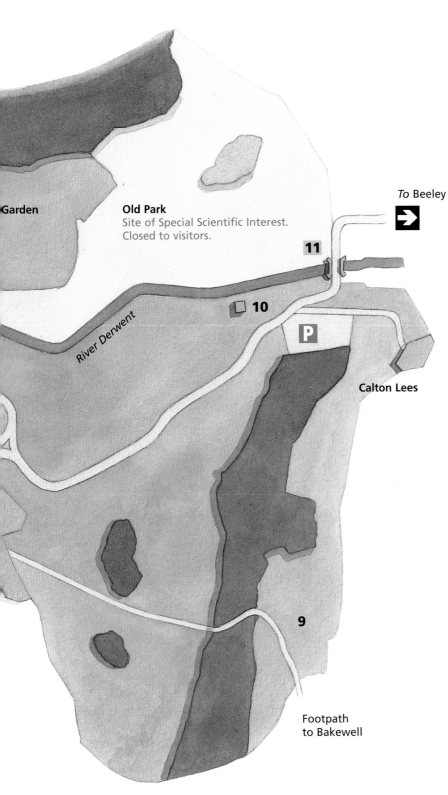

Garden

Old Park
Site of Special Scientific Interest.
Closed to visitors.

To Beeley

11

□ 10

P

River Derwent

Calton Lees

9

Footpath
to Bakewell

11

One Arch Bridge

10

Paine's Mill

9

Calton Pastures

Sheep

Red deer

PARK
MAP

Elizabethan Chatsworth (top).
Hardwick New Hall built by Bess
after Chatsworth (middle).
The Hunting Tower; a banqueting
house and vantage point to view
the deer hunt (above).

William Senior's 1617 survey of Chatsworth and its park.

1 River Derwent

2 Fish ponds

3 Queen Mary's Bower

4 Warren

5 House

6 Hunting Tower

7 Park

8 Roads to Chesterfield

Chatsworth's first park occupied the steep slope and high ground behind the house. Bess of Hardwick was born in Derbyshire, bought Hardwick Old Hall, and persuaded her second husband, Sir William Cavendish, to buy Chatsworth in 1549. She lived at Chatsworth while he spent time at the Royal court in London, a six day journey away. Derbyshire was a wild and isolated place. Bess built a new house and tamed the landscape around it for the production of food, from fruit in the orchards, to carp in the fish ponds, rabbits in the warren and deer in the park. The park was also a status symbol, a place for hunting and recreation and a site for timber production.

HUNTING TOWER   106

"Mary Queen of Scots was brought to Chatsworth several times as Queen Elizabeth I's prisoner. There is an unproven story that she used this platform, 'Queen Mary's Bower', as an exercise ground."

Christine Robinson, Head Housekeeper

'Capability' Brown (far left).

James Paine (middle left).

Paine's Bridge (left).

Chatsworth in about 1770,
painted by William Marlow.

1 Paine's Bridge
2 Hunting Tower
3 Stables
4 Cascade
5 River Derwent

The 4th Duke of Devonshire swept away the working landscape to create a new less formal park. Much of the formal gardens around the house had already been removed by the 3rd Duke. He hired Lancelot 'Capability' Brown (1716-83) to create an imposing man-made setting for the house, but one that gave the illusion of 'natural' countryside. Brown's vast schemes of earth movement and tree-planting took more than eight years and involved 25,000 man days of labour. He modified the course of the River Derwent and demolished the part of Edensor village within view of the house. James Paine (1717-89) designed the new bridges, the stable block and water mill.

FORMAL GARDEN	72
STABLES	98

"This landscape was farmed for many centuries before 'Capability' Brown created the park. The system of ploughing used by medieval farmers has left its shadow in the form of earthworks, called 'ridge and furrow'."

David Spencer, Domain Supervisor

13

Fallow deer (far left).
The International Horse Trials
taking place in the park (left).

A view west from the house across the park.

The park covers 400 hectares and is enclosed by a nine mile long dry stone wall and deer fence. It is home to red and fallow deer, sheep, cattle and many wild animals. Without the work of Chatsworth staff it would soon be changed beyond recognition by nature and the wear and tear caused by the footfall of a million visitors each year. Members of the **domain** team maintain all the trees, walls, railings, fences, watercourses, roads, tracks, gates, cattle grids, tree guards and an intricate system of underground drains. They also collect litter, which is dangerous to the animals that live in the park. The 76 hectare Old Park is a Site of Special Scientific Interest and is kept private to protect wildlife.

"Heading off on horseback gives me a different angle from which to view the park. I took this photograph during one morning ride."

The Duchess of Devonshire

WELCOME TO THE HOUSE

North Wing
Pages 58-67

Guest Bedrooms
Page 52-53

Sketch Galleries
Pages 46-51

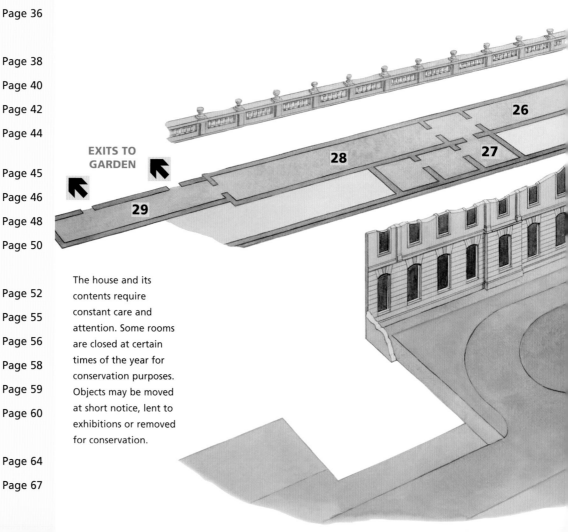

EXITS TO GARDEN

The house and its contents require constant care and attention. Some rooms are closed at certain times of the year for conservation purposes. Objects may be moved at short notice, lent to exhibitions or removed for conservation.

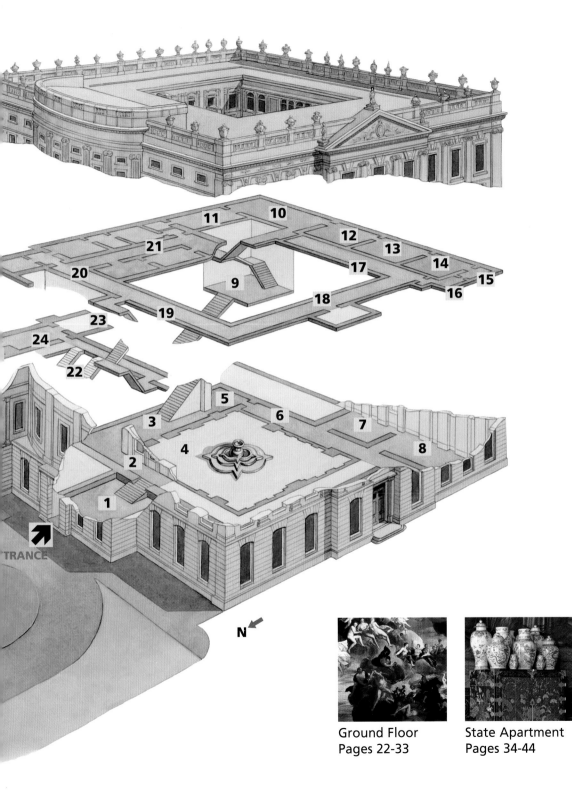

ENTRANCE

N

Ground Floor
Pages 22-33

State Apartment
Pages 34-44

The Devonshire Collection is the creation of one family over sixteen generations. It has evolved, and continues to grow, out of their tastes, passions and inheritance. From the smallest engraved gem to the largest outdoor sculpture, the objects are as varied as the personalities of the family members who collected them.

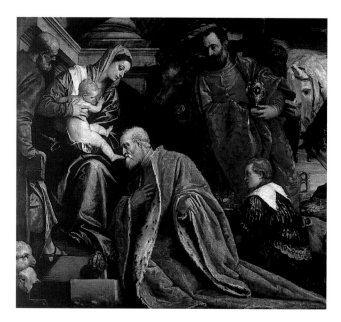

They include royal gifts, and discoveries made on the **Grand Tour** of Europe.

Many, like this painting (left) by Cornelis de Vos (1584-1681) once furnished other houses owned by the family, such as Devonshire House in London (below).

The first serious collector in the family was the 2nd Duke of Devonshire who purchased many **Old Master** drawings and paintings, including the Adoration of the Magi (above) by Paolo Veronese (1528-88).

In 1748, two great family collections were united by the marriage of the future 4th Duke and Lady Charlotte Boyle, daughter of the architect and collector, the 3rd Earl of Burlington. The Burlington Inheritance included Burlington House and Chiswick House (left) in London, and all their contents.

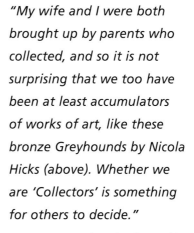

The 5th Duke and Duchess Georgiana commissioned portraits from eminent artists such as Sir Joshua Reynolds (1723-92), a tradition continued by the 11th Duke of Devonshire and Duchess Deborah with artists including Lucian Freud (1922-2011) and Pietro Annigoni (1910-88) (above).

In scale, no-one had more impact than the 6th Duke, a connoisseur of books and sculpture and a magpie collector of fascinating objects, from a jewelled hawk (below) and gold dog collars, to King Henry VIII's rosary.

"My wife and I were both brought up by parents who collected, and so it is not surprising that we too have been at least accumulators of works of art, like these bronze Greyhounds by Nicola Hicks (above). Whether we are 'Collectors' is something for others to decide."

The Duke of Devonshire

PORTRAITS

- **Georgiana, Duchess of Devonshire, by Thomas Gainsborough,** *c.* **1784**
- **The 6th Duke of Devonshire,** *c.* **1852**

Portraits are a method of recording and displaying family history. The 5th Duke and Georgiana commissioned the most famous artists of their time to paint their portraits. Their son was the first Duke of Devonshire to have his photograph taken, soon after the technique had been invented.

PAINTINGS

- **Trial by Jury, by Sir Edwin Landseer,** *c.* **1840**

This is one of hundreds of paintings in the Devonshire Collection. When the 6th Duke bought it he asked Landseer to add the Duke's own pet spaniel, Bony, to the left of the French poodle.

SCULPTURE

- **Sculpture Gallery, designed by Sir Jeffry Wyatville, completed by 1832**

The sculpture collection in the house, garden and park spans over 4000 years. The 6th Duke built a new gallery to display his collection, with innovative skylights and locally quarried sandstone walls to set off the marble sculptures.

FURNITURE

- **Seaweed marquetry cabinet, by Gerreit Jensen,** *c.* **1690-95**

Different generations of the family have bought furniture from the finest craftsmen of their time. Jensen, royal cabinet-maker to four English monarchs, made furniture such as this cabinet for the 1st Duke.

PRECIOUS METALS

• **Silver chandelier, 1690s**
The 1st Duke spent vast amounts of money on silver and silver-gilt objects. They are rare survivals, as it was common to melt down precious metals and remake them into new fashionable objects.

CERAMICS

• **Delft flower pyramid, c.1690**
The 1st Duke and Duchess began Chatsworth's ceramics collection with items of blue and white **Delftware**, made fashionable by their friend Queen Mary II.

BOOKS

• **Illustrated manuscript, 1465-68**
There are over 30,000 books at Chatsworth, from illuminated manuscripts on vellum (calfskin) to the great illustrated botanical books of the 19th century.

MINERALS

• **Amethyst**
Duchess Georgiana began a family tradition of mineral collecting in the 1780s. Duchess Deborah gave this amethyst geode to the 11th Duke as a Christmas present.

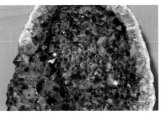

TEXTILES

• **Tapestry, Mortlake works, c.1695**
Chatsworth has many textiles in its collection and its own team of textile conservators.

CHATSWORTH IS HOME TO AN IMMENSE VARIETY OF TREASURES, LINKED BY THE SINGLE THREAD OF THE CAVENDISH FAMILY.

Bronze dog by Philip Blacker (below).
Bolton Abbey in Olden Times, by Sir Edwin Landseer (1802-73) (bottom).

12 | 4th DUKE'S PARK

This entrance hall was once the kitchen, positioned on the north side of the house to keep it cool. Visitors originally entered through the West Door, which is now the family's private entrance. The 4th Duke created this entrance hall when he redirected the approach to Chatsworth in the 1760s. He built a new wing for his kitchens, a forerunner of the 6th Duke's north wing.

The North Sub Corridor was once an open colonnade which sheltered visitors as they walked across the courtyard.

The 6th Duke bought the marble pavement (below) in Rome, having enclosed the colonnade to make it less draughty, improving the overall comfort for his guests. The colourful marble was intended to distract visitors from the fact that the door into the courtyard is not in the centre of the corridor.

Mahogany chair designed by William Kent (*c.*1685-1748) for Chiswick House (above).

6th DUKE'S HOUSE   54

The Duke chose stories from **classical** mythology that would flatter King William and Queen Mary to cover the painted walls and ceilings.

The 1st Duke initially only planned to rebuild the south front, but this triggered a passion for building. The illustration (left) shows how the old west front and new south front co-existed for a time.

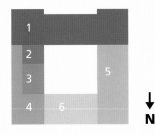

N

1687-89 South Front

1688-89 Great Stairs

1689-91 Painted Hall

1693-95 East Front

1699-1702 West Front

1705-07 North Front

"Because the 1st Duke was so haphazard in his rebuilding, the west front is actually longer than the east and the south-east corner is higher than the north-west."

Sean Doxey, Head of Special Projects

The 1st Duke spent twenty years rebuilding the Elizabethan house, which had become old-fashioned and was unstable when he inherited it. He earned his title by helping bring King William III (1650-1702) and Queen Mary II (1662-94) to the English throne during the **Glorious Revolution** of 1688. By the time of his death he had turned Chatsworth into a palace fit for a royal visit, but to his disappointment William and Mary never visited. The Duke was helped by the architects William Talman (1650-1719) and Thomas Archer (1668-1743) and possibly designed the west front himself. He devoted an entire suite of rooms, the State Apartment, for the King and Queen to use, and covered many walls and ceilings with symbolic paintings to flatter them. He was inspired by the grandest European palaces at the time which were **Baroque**, a theatrical style of architecture designed to amaze visitors and impress them with his cosmopolitan taste.

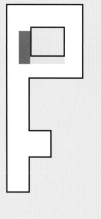

Louis Laguerre (top).
Laguerre's signature on the wall (centre).
The 1st Duke's alabaster staircase had Blue John mineral between each step (bottom).

The 1st Duke's guests would have crossed the courtyard to reach the Painted Hall. Replacing Bess of Hardwick's Great Hall, this was the first step in the journey to the State Apartment. The murals show scenes from the life of the Roman ruler Julius Caesar (100-44 BC) painted by Louis Laguerre (1663-1721). Visitors then would have recognised these as a tribute to King William III, England's new military hero. In 1779 the 5th Duke of Devonshire and Duchess Georgiana replaced the gritstone floor with black and white marble. The 6th Duke later added the ground floor windows and two galleries and replaced the steep double staircase with a more gentle single flight. He admitted that "the former steps here were decidedly more handsome". In 1912 the 9th Duke of Devonshire and Duchess Evelyn built the present staircase, retaining a single gallery. Before ascending to the State Apartment, visitors today see the 1st Duke's Grotto and Chapel.

"The house is filled with illusions in the painted decorations, paintings and carvings, which all add to the **Baroque** sense of theatre."

Matthew Hirst, Head of Art and Historic Collections

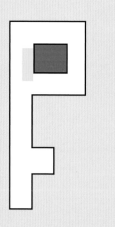

Every visitor to the 1st Duke's house would cross this courtyard. It originally had two open colonnades, carvings on every side, statues in niches and pea green painted columns. The four surviving military carvings, or trophies, were carved by the local sculptor Samuel Watson (1663-1715). In 2009 the stonework was cleaned, repaired and restored after 300 years of exposure to weathering and pollution.

The 6th Duke enclosed the open colonnades (below), 'adding warmth to the house and raising a second gallery'.

The Grotto was central to the 1st Duke's unusually modern supply of hot and cold running water. The same supply of water from the moors now feeds Chatsworth's fountains, flushes its lavatories and powers its electricity turbines. The **bas-relief** (left) shows Diana, the Roman goddess of hunting and the moon. In Roman mythology a mortal, Actaeon, saw Diana bathing after a hunt. She punished him by turning him into a stag.

"Our son, William, commissioned a digital portrait of his wife, Laura, by American artist Michael Craig-Martin. The colours constantly change and the portrait will never look the same twice."

The Duchess of Devonshire

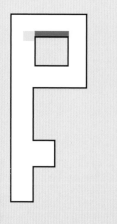

18   COLLECTING

Edmund de Waal (below) made 'a sounding line' for Chatsworth in 2006-7 (bottom).

This corridor brings together paintings, minerals and sculpture collected by several generations. Flower paintings by Jean-Baptiste Monnoyer (1636-99) show the splendour of the 1st Duke's **baroque** style. Two statues of Sekhmet, the Egyptian goddess of war, were collected by the 6th Duke and are 3,000 years old. They are joined by Old Master paintings, Greek, Roman and later sculpture as well as contemporary ceramics.

The oak panelling in this room is from a German monastery; notice the intricate carvings and busts of cardinals and bishops. The 6th Duke bought the panels at a London auction not knowing where he would place them until he returned home. He considered after the event 'so inconsiderate a purchase was never made – however look at the result. Is it not charming?'

The 6th Duke was a man with eclectic tastes and inserted paintings of his favourite dogs and views of Northumbrian and Italian holidays in the panels of the oak.

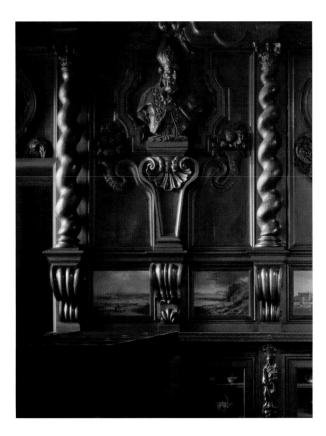

The 6th Duke's dogs (top) and Prior's Haven, Tynemouth, by John Wilson Carmichael (1800-68) (above).

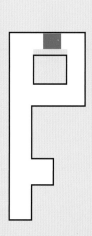

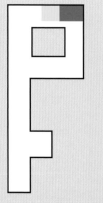

This Protestant Chapel has hardly changed since the 1st Duke built it in 1687-93. The figures of Faith and Justice on either side of the altarpiece were carved by Caius Gabriel Cibber (1630-1700). They represent the balance between church and state, which the Duke believed to be under threat from the Roman Catholic King James II (1633-1701). The Duke helped to overthrow the King during the **Glorious Revolution** of 1688. The image of Christ healing the sick painted opposite the windows by Louis Laguerre may symbolise England's return to religious health after the Glorious Revolution. The local sculptor Samuel Watson carved the alabaster altarpiece and cedar wood panels. Antonio Verrio (1639-1707) painted 'Doubting Thomas' above the altar table, which had two prayer books for use during services.

Detail of the cedar wood carvings (top).
Detail of the altarpiece and wall painting (bottom).

"We see the Chapel many times every
day from the gallery, and it has become
my favourite room to look at. We use
the Chapel on special occasions, such
as the christening of our grand-
daughter Maud Cavendish."

The Duchess of Devonshire

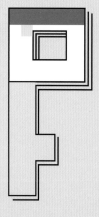

An 'honesty square' shows how dark the walls of the Great Stairs had become before they were cleaned in 1997-8 (middle). The 1st Duke's formal garden (above) was built to be viewed by the King and Queen from the State Apartment.

These stairs lead to the State Apartment, the most important rooms in the 1st Duke's house. He built this series of rooms for King William III and Queen Mary II to use on a royal visit. As in royal palaces, this would be a public space and strict rules would control how far a person could progress down the **enfilade** of rooms to the King and Queen. Each is more private and ornate than the last. The staircase is designed to build suspense as visitors ascend to the State Apartment. They are cantilevered, "so artfully contriv'd that they seem to hang in the Air", (Dr Charles Leigh, 1700). Jean Tijou (active 1689-1712), ironworker to William III, made the gilded iron **balustrade**. Verrio's painted ceiling flows into Watson's carvings on the upper parts of the walls, where the Duke abandoned murals for garden sculptures by Cibber.

"This engraving shows what a royal visit might have been like. But in the end William and Mary never came to Chatsworth. The 1st Duke must have been incredibly disappointed."

Christine Robinson, Head Housekeeper

The Great Chamber is the largest room in the State Apartment. If the expected royal visit had taken place it would have been busy with people wanting an audience with the King and Queen. Few would have been allowed to progress beyond this room. Stools with velvet cushions and gold trimmings once stood against the walls. The focus now is a buffet, a pyramid of silver-gilt and porcelain dishes displaying the 1st Duke's wealth and taste.

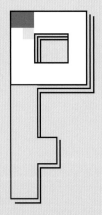

The buffet (top).

Verrio's painted ceiling (detail) (above).

*"This flower pyramid has holders to display flowers from the garden. Queen Mary II introduced the fashion for these **Delftware** vases from the town of Delft in Holland."*

Hannah Obee, Curator of Decorative Art

WOOD CARVING

The 1st Duke's accounts show that he bought about 18 tonnes of oak panelling for the State Apartment. Watson carved the fish, game birds, fruit and flowers in lime wood. The theme of food suggests that this room may have been intended for occasional banquets. The lime wood was once almost silver in colour, in contrast to the dark oak.

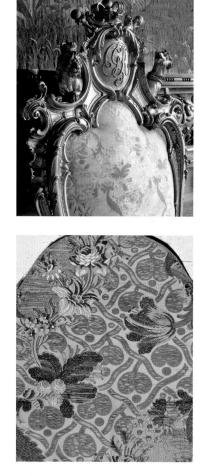

Important courtiers would have 'withdrawn' to the State Drawing Room from the Great Chamber. The walls are hung with tapestries made in around 1635 by Flemish weavers at the Mortlake works in London. They show scenes of the Acts of the Apostles taken from drawings by Raphael (1483-1520). King George III (1738-1820) and Queen Charlotte (1744-1818) used the two thrones at their coronation and gave them to the 4th Duke, their Lord Chamberlain, as a perquisite (perk) of the job.

A throne, upholstered in silk enriched with silver thread (top). Back of throne (above). A tapestry, made from silk and wool, in storage (detail) (right).

"Textiles fade over the centuries. These pictures of the back of one of the thrones and a tapestry that has been kept in storage show how colourful this room once looked."

Susie Stokoe,
Textiles Department Supervisor

GLOBAL INFLUENCES

These cabinets and coffers are made from lacquer, produced from the sap of a tree which only grows in China, Korea and Japan. This type of furniture became known as coromandel because it was imported via the Indian port on the Coromandel coast. Groups of Chinese porcelain are crowded on top of the furniture. Displays like this showed the wealth of a collector who owned rare porcelain before the secret of its production was discovered in Europe in 1708.

This was a second withdrawing room intended for the King and Queen's most trusted courtiers. The 6th Duke renamed it the Music Room after he brought the violin door here from Devonshire House in London. The violin is a trompe l'oeil, or trick of the eye, painted by the Dutch artist Jan van der Vaardt (*c.*1653-1727). The 6th Duke also replaced green velvet wall hangings with cuir repoussé (stamped and gilded leather) containing nine leather portraits of himself in the frieze.

Violin door (detail) (top). Cuir repoussé portrait of the 6th Duke (right).

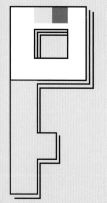

"The 6th Duke wrote a Handbook of Chatsworth in 1844. Of these leather portraits, he wrote, 'There are many things at Chatsworth that I should not have allowed myself to do...'"

Andrew Peppitt, Archivist

BOULLE FURNITURE

This furniture was made by the Frenchman André-Charles Boulle (1642-1732), or in his style. As Louis XIV's (1638-1715) cabinet-maker, Boulle perfected a new technique of gluing together sheets of turtle shell and brass. He cut out a pattern using a fret-saw and combined the sheets to produce a turtle shell background with a brass design and a brass background with a turtle shell design. Turtle shell came from India and the West Indies and was highly sought after.

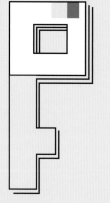

The Gumley mirror (below).
Diana on the ceiling (below right).
The silver-gilt toilet service
belonged to Queen Mary II
(bottom).

An inner circle of attendants would have waited on the King or Queen in this bedroom. The State Bed is not the original one made for the room, but it is the same age. In 2005 a group of specialists discovered that its canopy had been lowered. They raised it back to its original height and covered the faded silk in a crimson net to protect it. New silk was woven for the window curtains to match the original bed hangings. The 1st Duke's costly mirror is signed 'John Gumley, 1703' on the central lower pane of mirror glass.

"The subject of the painted ceiling is appropriate for a bedroom because it shows Aurora, Roman goddess of the dawn, waiting to chase away Diana, goddess of the moon, or night."

Charles Noble, Curator of Fine Art

PRECIOUS METALS

Silver and gold objects were used to display wealth, but also had
practical uses. Their intrinsic value meant that they could be melted
down and re-used in hard times. They were strong and durable and
also reflected precious candle light into dark rooms. The silver
perfume burner (right) would have helped mask the smells created by
large gatherings of people and banquets during a royal visit.

39 COROMANDEL

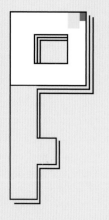

If they had visited, the King and Queen would have carried out their most important business here. The few people allowed in would have left by walking backwards through the **enfilade** of rooms. Mirrors at each end make the enfilade seem longer than it really is. The 1st Duke originally covered these walls in coromandel lacquer panels which he later re-used to make pieces of furniture, including the chest to the left of the fireplace. The quantity of rare porcelain in this room would have impressed visitors with the family's taste and social standing.

"The 9th Duke and Duchess Evelyn added the fireplace and hung the 1st Duke's silver chandelier in the 1920s. Evelyn wrote, 'a cloud is an unsubstantial thing from which to hang a very heavy object, but it does not do to be hypercritical'."

Matthew Hirst,
Head of Art and Historic Collections

Old Master Drawings are on display at Chatsworth for the first time in over a century. The collection of drawings is considered to be the greatest private collection in the country, after the Royal Collection. There are over 3000 drawings by artists including Leonardo da Vinci, Raphael, Rembrandt and Guercino. The majority of the drawings were collected by the 2nd Duke of Devonshire and his son, the 3rd Duke, in the 18th century. The temporary exhibitions of drawings are displayed in a small room designed to resemble an 18th century collector's cabinet - a private space for the display and contemplation of highly prized works of art. On permanent display is Rembrandt's portrait of an Oriental, purchased by the 3rd Duke in 1742, and a rare 17th-century Florentine cabinet decorated with pietra dura panels.

Portrait of an Oriental (King Uzziah) by Rembrandt, c.1639 (top).
A man sculling a boat on the Bullewijk, with a view toward Ouderkerk by Rembrandt, c.1650 (above).
A thatched cottage by a large tree, a figure seated outside by Rembrandt, c.1648-52 (left).

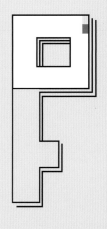

This gallery is filled with objects collected by the 5th Duke and Duchess Georgiana. Georgiana was a source of inspiration in political campaigning, fashion and collecting. She was an early enthusiast of mineral collecting, and a friend of Marie Antoinette (1755-93), Queen of France. Their friendship helped to promote French tastes in art, dress and furniture in England. Georgiana and the Duke lived in a ménage-à-trois with her friend Lady Elizabeth Foster, who married the Duke after Georgiana's death. The present Duke and Duchess redisplayed and extended the Sketch Galleries in 2009, when many of the objects in this gallery were conserved.

28   COURTYARD

A photographic montage of Georgiana as the Goddess Diana by Maria Cosway (1760-1838) before and after conservation in 2009 (above).
Keira Knightley as Duchess Georgiana during filming of The Duchess at Chatsworth in 2008 (right).

"Members of staff and Friends of Chatsworth signed the walls before they were covered with silk. The house has many hidden signatures, some are 300 years old."

Simon Seligman, former Head of Communications

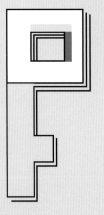

Portrait of Richard Boyle, 3rd Earl of Burlington by George Knapton (top). Portrait of William Kent by Benedetto Luti (above). Chiswick House, London (right).

This gallery celebrates the collection of the 3rd Earl of Burlington also known as 'the architect Earl'. His daughter, Lady Charlotte Boyle, married the 4th Duke and their son, the 5th Duke, inherited the collections of both families. Lord Burlington revolutionised English architecture in the **Palladian** style, inspired by the Italian architect Andrea Palladio (1508-80).

The 3rd Earl of Burlington designed his own home, Chiswick House, in the Palladian style which included strict observations of symmetry and proportion. In 1929, the 9th Duke of Devonshire finally sold Chiswick House. The 3rd Earl of Burlington championed William Kent, who designed landscapes, interiors and furnishings, including the tables and chairs on display. His portrait can be found at the far end of the gallery.

"We have placed Lord Burlington's portrait between busts of his heroes, the Italian architect Palladio and the English architect Inigo Jones."

Charles Noble, Curator

49

In 2013 this gallery will host two exhibitions. The first, from March to June will showcase paintings, drawings and sculpture by post-war British artist William Turnbull (1922-2012). Turnbull was a member of the Independent Group, based at the Institute of Contemporary Art (ICA), London, in the 1950s, that also included Richard Hamilton and Eduardo Paolozzi, and he was an early friend of the American Abstract Expressionists Mark Rothko and Barnett Newman. This exhibition is part of a larger display of his sculpture in the garden during the spring of 2013.

William Turnbull with pieces of his own art work photographed by Jorge Lewinski.

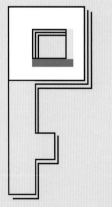

NORTH SKETCH GALLERY

The second part of the year will host an exhibition of pieces chosen from the Duke and Duchess' own private collection. The North Sketch Gallery, created in 2009, is unlike its counterparts. This gallery has been created in order to show contemporary art and ceramics. The gallery displays change throughout the season. If you would like to know any more information about the artwork currently on display please speak to the room guides or refer to the room cards.

GUEST BEDROOMS

A 1906 shooting party at Chatsworth. The 8th Duke is standing sixth from the left. The Duchess is seated fourth from the left, next to King Edward VII (1841-1910) (above).
Princess Victoria (1819-1901) slept in this State Bed. Duchess Evelyn removed the canopy, stating that everyone who slept under it fell ill with a cold (top).

In 1830 the 6th Duke began to convert this part of the house into fashionable new guest bedrooms. This period saw the rise of the English country house party. These gatherings revolved around pleasure. During the day, guests could choose from amusements including hunting, shooting, reading, drawing, music and billiards. Formal evening dinners were followed by music, charades, performances and smoking for the men. Women might return to their bedroom up to six times a day to change their clothes, never wearing the same outfit twice during their visit. Today this is the most complete set of bedrooms from the period to survive with their original furnishings. The hand-painted Chinese wallpaper and sugar-glazed chintz fabric are typical of Regency taste, which developed during the reign of George IV (1762-1830) first as Regent then as King. It is characterised by vivid colours, eastern influences and decorative patterns. The light levels are kept low to protect the delicate materials.

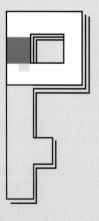

"People who have stayed at Chatsworth include Queen Victoria (right), the 1st Duke of Wellington and Charles Dickens."

Christine Robinson, Head Housekeeper

The proposed railing between the present great Piers line of railing about 60 feet back from R and extending from the House towards the South would be in similar line, making the whole line of Gilt Railing about One Thousand feet. Railing of the Extreme Screen 150 feet back from S. Sunwell Wall about 20 feet high and in height from T 65 feet upon which space between the two last letters the Carriage is supposed to be passing.

West Front

W The Stewards Offices about 45 feet back from V
X The back wall of the Offices shall also of the moved way above to the Stables is about 70 feet back from W
Y Is the end of the Kitchen Building the lower building is the Larder which is intended to stop the Wall between the appearance of an unbroken line and yet of a large size & the Stewards Office line from the two.
Z The House at the back of the dining room shall the Windows Parlors for to live with those of the Mansion.

THE 6th DUKE'S HOUSE

The 6th Duke spent 20 years improving and enlarging Chatsworth. Entertaining was a social responsibility he took very seriously, and he modernised the 1st Duke's house to meet new standards of comfort. This also created more space for his growing collections. In 1818 he began altering the existing rooms to reflect his taste, and he went on to build an entire new north wing. An idea to build a symmetrical wing to the south was abandoned. His architect, Sir Jeffry Wyatville (1766-1840), painted the watercolour of Chatsworth pictured above.

Jeffry Wyatt (below), later Sir Jeffry Wyatville, had worked at Longleat and went on to work for King George IV at Windsor Castle.

Here are portraits of the 1st to the 11th Dukes and some of their family and friends. The 6th Duke turned four floors of rooms into this single staircase, crowned by a dome and lantern, to lead to his new north wing. After alterations in the 1920s, the present Duke and Duchess restored the staircase to its original appearance in 2009.

This group portrait of Ladies Alexandra, Mary and Theodosia Acheson, granddaughters of Louise, Duchess of Devonshire by her first marriage to the 7th Duke of Manchester, was painted by John Singer Sargent (1856-1925). Sargent initially wanted to draw the ladies as they played a game of golf, however this conventional composition was chosen.

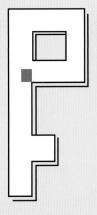

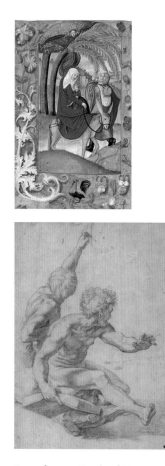

The 6th Duke turned the 1st Duke's long gallery into a library. There are over 30,000 books at Chatsworth. Each generation has added to the collection, which contains rare illuminated manuscripts and **incunabula**. It includes most of the original works of the philosopher Thomas Hobbes (1588-1679), who tutored the 2nd and 3rd Earls. The 2nd Duke collected drawings and prints by **Old Masters**, including Raphael, Rembrandt and Sir Anthony van Dyck (1599-1641), and stored them in albums. The 4th Duke inherited Lord Burlington's architectural library. The 6th Duke was a great lover of books and purchased entire libraries. He collected illustrated natural history books, as did the 7th and 11th Dukes.

Page from a Book of Hours According to the Use of Sarum, given to Margaret Tudor by her father King Henry VII, c.1500 (top). Nude studies for St. Andrew and another apostle in The Transfiguration, by Raphael, c.1517 (above). Illustration from The Birds of America, by John James Audubon (1827-39) (right).

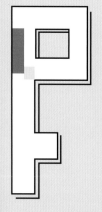

"Sometimes I am asked how people get up to the gallery in the Library. There is a hidden 'book door' which leads to a spiral stone staircase in the wall."

The Duke of Devonshire

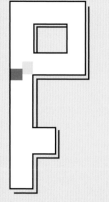

'The Book of Lismore'
15th century (below).
Book bound by the Geometrical
Compartment Binder 1710-1720
(bottom).

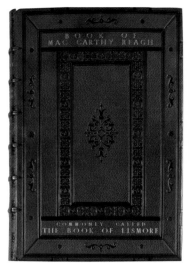

This is one of three smaller library rooms at Chatsworth. The 1st Duke used it as a dining room, then a billiard room. The 6th Duke believed windows of a single pane of glass to be "the greatest ornament of modern decoration". He installed many, including all the windows on the south front, replacing the original sash windows. Only this example of the 6th Duke's new windows now remains. The room contains many books from the library of the scientist, Henry Cavendish (1731-1810), the 'first man to weigh the world'.

King Henry VIII after
Hans Holbein the Younger
(*c.*1497-1543) (above).

This is where the 6th Duke's north wing begins. His **enfilade** of rooms leads away for 128 metres to the north and south. He used it to gather his guests before dinner, and wrote, "I find that most formal, weariest, hungriest moment of life less painful when the patients are squeezed together in a small compass; there is less space for their ceremonies, their shyness, and their awkwardness".

The 6th Duke commissioned the marble Veiled Vestal Virgin by Raffaelle Monti (1818-81) in 1846. The vestals were the priestesses of Vesta, goddess of Earth who looked over the sacred flame in ancient Rome. The flame represented the security of Rome and was never allowed to go out (right).

A Christmas menu from the early 20th century (below).

In this recreated Victorian table setting (bottom), the cutlery would be used from the outside inwards for each successive course.

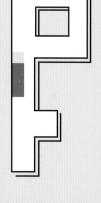

The first dinner to be held here was for the 13-year-old Princess Victoria. It was her first adult dinner and there was a cooked rehearsal the day before. The 6th Duke wrote, "it is like dining in a giant trunk and you expect the lid to open". He brought portraits by van Dyck from his other houses to hang on the walls. In 1996-2001, Chatsworth's textile team replaced the damaged silk on the walls and made new window curtains, exact copies of the 6th Duke's. The Duke and Duchess host dinners here on very special occasions.

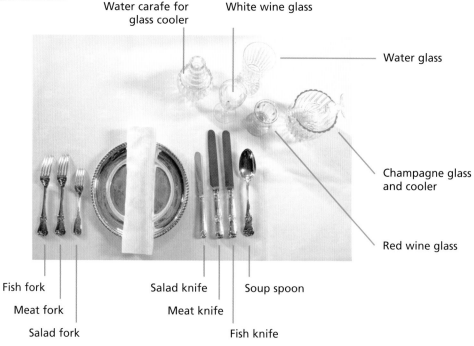

Water carafe for glass cooler

White wine glass

Water glass

Champagne glass and cooler

Red wine glass

Fish fork

Meat fork

Salad fork

Salad knife

Meat knife

Fish knife

Soup spoon

"To care for the silver collection at Chatsworth we have careful routines for monitoring, handling and cleaning. Pieces on show such as the silver in the dining room require regular removal of surface dust. We do this by light cleaning with tarnish inhibiting cloths."

Ellin Belton, Collections Steward

Formal dining has been at the heart of life in grand houses for centuries. A large meal, served in the Great Dining Room, was the result of an extensive process behind the scenes. A wide range of staff, expertise and resources was needed to prepare food and serve guests with suitable magnificence.

THE FOOD

Food and drink came from the estate's farms, woods, deer park and rivers, and from specialist suppliers. In an age before refrigerators, ice was made in ice houses (below) in the garden and park.

THE KITCHEN

The varied skills of successive head cooks and their teams were needed to ensure the kitchens (left) were as self-sufficient as possible, producing elaborate dishes for the family and their guests, and feeding the staff.

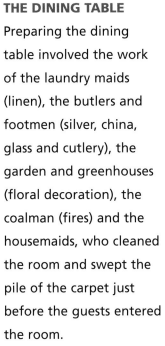

THE STAFF

Serving guests was the work of the butlers and footmen, in full livery and powdered hair.

THE DINING TABLE

Preparing the dining table involved the work of the laundry maids (linen), the butlers and footmen (silver, china, glass and cutlery), the garden and greenhouses (floral decoration), the coalman (fires) and the housemaids, who cleaned the room and swept the pile of the carpet just before the guests entered the room.

THE DINNER

The picture above shows a dinner held in the Great Dining Room in 1897, hosted by the 8th Duke (1) and Duchess Louise (2) for the future King Edward VII (3) and Queen Alexandra (1844-1925) (4).

"Colour in the Sculpture Gallery was very important to the 6th Duke. He set brightly coloured panels of carefully chosen rare minerals into some of the sculptures' plinths."

Charles Noble, Curator of Fine Art

Canova (below).
Pope Clement XIII's tomb
(bottom), an arrangement
recreated at the far end of the
gallery (left).

This gallery contains the 6th Duke's contemporary sculptures, which were modern art when he collected them.

The Duke commissioned this top-lit gallery for the sculptures, which are mostly in a **classical** style, with gritstone walls to emphasise the marble. From the age of 28 until his death, aged 68, he was a compulsive collector of sculpture. He visited Italy and met some of the best artists of his time. He became great friends with the famous sculptor Antonio Canova (1757-1822) and this gallery could be seen as a shrine to the artist. The Duke positioned busts of himself and Canova above copies of two lions Canova had made for the tomb of Pope Clement XIII (1536-1605) at St Peter's in Rome.

SCULPTURE 96

To make a marble sculpture, Canova would have begun by drawing sketches, then making a small clay model to perfect the composition before creating full size versions in plaster. Next would follow months of hard physical labour carving the stone. Mistakes were costly, and it was impossible to know whether a block of marble might be flawed inside. Canova was admired for carving his sculptures himself, whilst other artists employed teams of carvers to work the stone.

This set of tools which Canova used to make clay models is on display in the Sculpture Gallery.

"After the 6th Duke died, different generations moved some of the sculptures to other parts of the house. In 2009 we finished the process of reuniting them and recreated the 6th Duke's arrangement down to the last inch."

Charles Noble, Curator of Fine Art

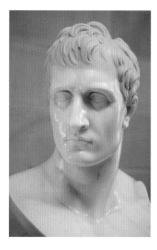

Napoleon Bonaparte (1769-1821), by Canova (top).

Pauline Borghese (1780-1825), Napoleon's sister (bottom).

Napoleon's first wife to Josephine de Beauharnais (1763-1814) sent orange trees from her palace at Malmaison to the 6th Duke, who placed them in the Orangery.

The Orangery once filled the north wing with the scent of orange trees and other sweet-smelling plants. Until the early 1900s it housed tender plants and sculpture. The 6th Duke wrote of the large vase in the centre of the room, "At first it was in the Gallery, then it was ordered to the Pleasure Ground... but, being wheeled thus far on its way, the effect was so beautiful... that it stopped short, and here remains". Today the Orangery is a shop and the way out into the garden.

GREENHOUSES   94

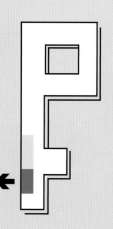

WELCOME TO THE GARDEN

If you are using a wheelchair or pushchair, please ask at the garden entrance for a leaflet showing all accessible paths.

○○○○○ Good paths and flat going

○○│○○ Various surfaces and slight gradients

1

Kitchen Garden, p.92

2

Flora's Temple, p.75

3

Display Greenhouse, p.94

4

1st Duke's Greenhouse, p.74

5

Cascade, p.76

6

Willow Tree Fountain, p.78

7

Ring Pond, p.79

8

Emperor Fountain, p.84

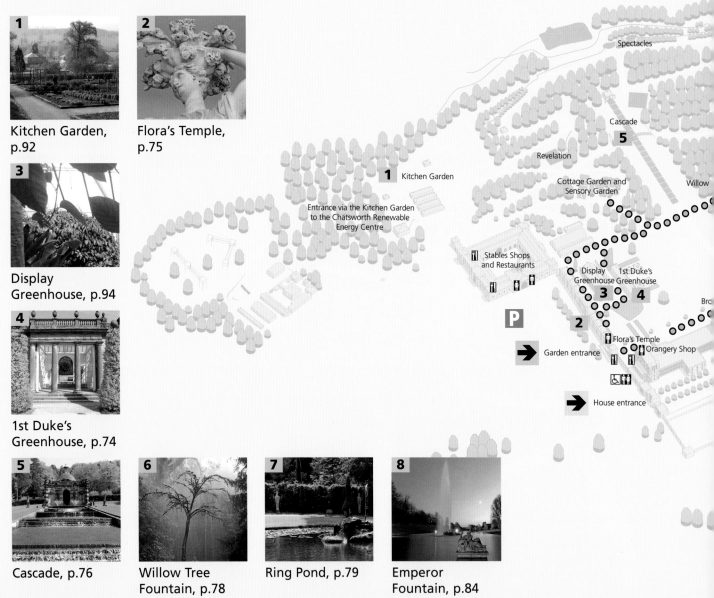

Spectacles

Cascade

5

Revelation

Cottage Garden and Sensory Garden

Willow

1 Kitchen Garden

Entrance via the Kitchen Garden to the Chatsworth Renewable Energy Centre

Stables Shops and Restaurants

Display Greenhouse

1st Duke's Greenhouse

Bro

3

4

P

2

Flora's Temple

Orangery Shop

Garden entrance

House entrance

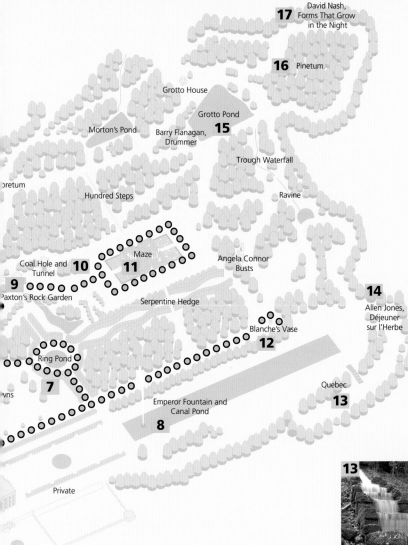

17 David Nash, Forms That Grow in the Night

16 Pinetum

Grotto House

Grotto Pond

Barry Flanagan, Drummer

15

Morton's Pond

Trough Waterfall

oretum

Ravine

Hundred Steps

Angela Connor Busts

Coal Hole and Tunnel

10

Maze

11

14

9

Allen Jones, Déjeuner sur l'Herbe

Paxton's Rock Garden

Serpentine Hedge

Blanche's Vase

12

Ring Pond

7

Quebec

13

wns

Emperor Fountain and Canal Pond

8

Private

17

Forms That Grow in the Night, p.89

16

Pinetum, p.88

15

Grotto Pond, p.88

13

Quebec, p.90

14

Déjeuner sur l'Herbe, p.96

9

Rockery, p.86

10

Coal Tunnel, p.83

11

Maze, p.82

12

Blanche's Vase

The garden is famous for its water features.

Rain [1] falling on the moor is drained by the **Emperor Stream [2]** and other man-made conduits into man-made **lakes [3]**.

Water from one lake, the Ring Pond, flows down over the **Sowter Stone and Aqueduct [4]**, a huge man-made water feature partly hidden in Stand Wood, and then underground to the Cascade Pond and down the **Cascade [5]**.

A pipe at the bottom of the Cascade feeds other fountains and carries water to flush **lavatories** in the house and stables [6].

Water from the Cascade Pond also flows to the **Wellington Rock and Strid Pond [7]** and the **Willow Tree Fountain [8]**, which both feed a second **Ring Pond [9]** in the garden.

Swiss Lake

Ring Pond

Emperor Lake

Aqueduct

Emperor pipe

Cascade Pond

Cascade

Stables

The **Emperor Fountain [10]** is fed directly from the Emperor Lake by an underground pipe. The pressure of the water dropping 122 metres through a pipe only 40 centimetres wide is enough to power the fountain to heights of up to 90 metres without using pumps. The water flows away down the **Quebec Cascade [11]**.

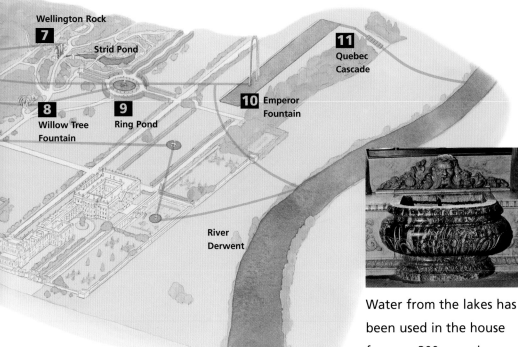

Wellington Rock
7
Strid Pond
11
Quebec Cascade
8
Willow Tree Fountain
9
Ring Pond
10 Emperor Fountain
River Derwent

THIS WATER CYCLE IS POWERED NOT BY PUMPS, BUT BY GRAVITY ALONE.

The Emperor pipe also feeds water-powered **turbines** which have supplied the house with electricity since 1893.

Water from the lakes has been used in the house for over 300 years in different ways, from filling the 1st Duke's marble bath and water-closets to powering Victorian kitchen and laundry machinery.

Kip and Knyff's view of
Chatsworth, 1699.

1 Queen Mary's Bower

2 1st Duke's Greenhouse

3 Palisade and trophies

4 Bowling House

5 Flora

6 Willow Tree Fountain

7 Cascade

8 Hunting Tower

Chatsworth c.1707 (below, far left),
and today (below left).
Hampton Court garden
(detail) (below).

The 1st Duke of Devonshire created a new formal garden, a statement of his taste and power. He hired the best European craftsmen to imitate King William III and Queen Mary II's garden at Hampton Court Palace and other royal gardens from across Europe. Every detail was planned to impress, in particular the view from the new State Apartment which had been built in the hope of a royal visit. The revival of **Classical** Greek and Roman ideas was highly fashionable across Europe, and influenced the Duke's choice of plants, sculptures, waterworks and the overall symmetry of the design. Today little remains of his garden. A new fashion for natural-looking landscape swept away the formal garden less than 50 years after it had been created. The large picture on the left shows how it looked in 1699. Some features depicted in this engraving have survived.

"Our camellias have won prizes at Royal Horticultural Society competitions every year since 1956. Chatsworth is the most northerly garden to enter camellias at their shows."

Ian Webster, former Head Gardener

Flora was the Roman goddess of flowers and springtime. The Flemish sculptor Jan Nost (d.1729) carved this sculpture for the 1st Duke in 1694. It originally stood where the Emperor Fountain is today. The temple was nearby and used as a bowling green house.

This greenhouse (left) is one of the oldest in England. King William III and Queen Mary II introduced the Dutch fashion for greenhouses and orangeries, which were named after the tender evergreens and oranges which grew inside them. The 1st Duke grew oranges, lemons and myrtles. The 4th Duke moved the greenhouse to its present position. Today it is open to visitors and used for growing prize-winning camellias.

Flora (top).
The 1st Duke's Greenhouse, Bowling House and Flora in 1699 (above).

"Water tricks were popular in the 1600s. The Duke could control sudden spurts of water through holes in the Temple floor to catch his guests by surprise. They still work!"

Matthew Hirst, Head of Art and Historic Collections

The Cascade and its Temple were the crowning point of the 1st Duke's garden.

It took two attempts and seventeen years before the arrangement was complete in 1711, four years after his death. He may have been inspired by the cascade at King Louis XIV's (1638-1715) French palace at Marly, which was also a model for the west front of the house. He hired an engineer, Grillet, who had designed waterworks for the French King. Thomas Archer, one of the Duke's architects, designed the temple. Another Frenchman, Henri Nadauld (d.1785), and Derbyshire-born Samuel Watson made the sculptural carvings. Each step in the Cascade is different, so that the sound of the water changes as it falls. The 6th Duke's Aqueduct can be seen in the woods above the Cascade, bringing water from the lakes into the garden.

The Cascade Temple (top).
The Cascade at Marly (middle).
The Pump Room behind the
Temple controls the gravity-fed
flow of water (right).

WATER 70

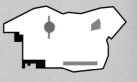

"The scale and complexity of the miles of underground pipes feeding the water features still amazes me, some are over 400 years old!"

Steve Porter,
Head of Gardens and Landscape

The Ring Pond lay in the middle of one of the 1st Duke's formal planted 'wildernesses'. The sculptures were made in the 1700s for Lord Burlington's garden at Chiswick. They are in the style of ancient Greek 'herms', which were believed to protect against evil spirits. The lead duck fountain was made in 1692. Its original home, now filled in, was known by Cavendish children as 'sick duck pond'.

The Willow Tree Fountain was a water trick made for the 1st Duke. It was originally in the Ring Pond and has been remade twice. The pioneering traveller Celia Fiennes (1662-1741) wrote in 1696, "all of a sudden by turning a sluce it raines from each leafe and from the branches like a shower, it being made of brass and pipes to each leafe but in appearance is exactly like a willow". Princess Victoria, aged thirteen, called it the 'squirting' tree.

The Ring Pond (top).
The herms at Chiswick (bottom).

"There are over 5 miles of hedges to trim every year. We have worked at night using lasers to shine a straight line, to make sure it's perfect."

Rob Dowding, Garden Supervisor

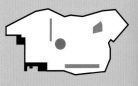

The Great Conservatory was Paxton's greatest achievement at Chatsworth. It stood where the maze is today.

The 6th Duke first encountered Joseph Paxton (1803-65) working in the garden of the Horticultural Society, next door to the Duke's London home at Chiswick. He appointed the promising 23-year-old as Chatsworth's Head Gardener. Paxton inspired the Duke with a passion for gardening and they became life-long friends, transforming the garden over the next 30 years. Thousands of people took advantage of the new railways to visit Chatsworth and see Paxton's feats of engineering, including the Emperor Fountain, Rockery and Great Conservatory. He went on to design the Crystal Palace in London, site of the 1851 Great Exhibition.

Paxton's revolutionary Crystal Palace in London (right). Inside the Great Conservatory (far left).
The banana *Musa acuminata* 'Dwarf Cavendish' was imported in 1829 and thrived at Chatsworth. It is now grown commercially around the world (centre left). Paxton also became an MP, architect, publisher and successful businessman (left).

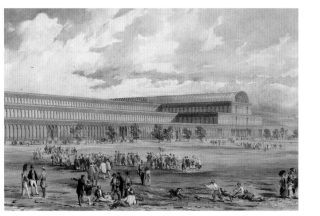

> *"Sometimes when we are digging here we still find fragments of the glass that fell when the conservatory was blown up."*
>
> Rob Dowding, Garden Supervisor

The 11th Duke and Duchess planted the maze with 1210 yew plants in 1962.

Its walls and paving were part of Paxton's Great Conservatory, once the largest glass building in the world. At Chatsworth Paxton discovered the secret to building large glass houses. He used light wooden frames with hollow iron columns for support and drainage and laid glass in a zigzag ridge-and-furrow system to absorb more sunlight. Every winter, horses and carts brought 300 tons of coal to fuel eight underground boilers and heat seven miles of hot water pipe to warm the exotic plants. The boiler fumes escaped through underground flues to a chimney on the hillside. During and after the First World War (1914-18), there was not enough coal to heat the conservatory and many plants died. It was demolished in 1920.

The hidden Coal Tunnel is open to visitors (top).
The chimney in Stand Wood (bottom).

"We turn on the fountain every morning. You have to lift a cover and use a four foot metal key to open the valve."

Glenn Facer, Gardener

This fountain can reach a height of 90 metres. It is powered by the pressure of the water dropping 122 metres, through a 40 centimetre iron pipe, from a man-made lake. The 1st Duke's Canal Pond already held the highest fountain in the country (28 metres) when Paxton began to engineer the Emperor Fountain for the 6th Duke in 1843. The 6th Duke had seen a 37 metre fountain in Russia belonging to his friend Tsar Nicholas I (1796-1855). When the Tsar announced a trip to England, Paxton's men worked day and night to finish it in time. They completed the fountain and dug a new lake to feed it in just six months. The Tsar never visited Chatsworth, but the fountain is named in his honour. It is usually only played to half its full height to conserve water.

WATER	70
PAXTON	80

Tsar Nicholas's fountain at Peterhof (above).
Penrhos College pupils skating on the Canal Pond while evacuated to Chatsworth during the Second World War (left).

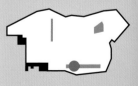

"In 1848, one of Paxton's gardeners, Robert Aughtie, wrote in his diary, 'finished the large Wellington Rock – had some ale in the evening to christen it – got rather tipsey and was very noisey coming home'."

Stuart Band, Archivist

This was one of the most ambitious rock gardens of its time and is entirely artificial. In 1838 the 6th Duke invited Paxton to join him on a **Grand Tour** of Europe and Paxton built the Rockery as a reminder of their journey through the Alps. He invented a steam-powered machine to lift the locally quarried gritstone rocks into position. Queen Victoria visited Chatsworth with Prince Albert and the Duke of Wellington in 1843 and the 6th Duke named three of the rock formations after them. Below the Rockery Paxton built the Strid, an imitation of the Strid at Bolton Abbey, the Duke's North Yorkshire estate. In 2007 the present Duchess planted a collection of dark or black flowers here called the Dark Side border.

PAXTON 80

The Dark Side (top).
A Swinging Rock near the Willow Tree Fountain, is now wedged in place for safety (bottom).
The Strid at Bolton Abbey (left).

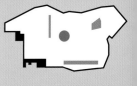

"At the entrance to the Pinetum is the 5th Duke and Georgiana's Grotto, with magnificent views from the 6th Duke's bandstand on top."

Steve Porter, Head of Gardens and Landscape

Here the 6th Duke indulged his passion for collecting on a grand scale. The 1820s was a time of great enthusiasm for plant-collecting and this was one of the first pinetums, or collections of coniferous trees, in England. It included a giant redwood, monkey puzzle, hemlock spruce and Japanese white pine. Paxton brought the seeds of the Douglas Fir (a species recently introduced from California) from London to Chatsworth wrapped in his hat. He perfected a technique for uprooting, transporting and re-planting fully grown trees. Chatsworth gardeners led global plant-hunting expeditions until 1838 when two of them, Robert Wallace and Peter Banks, drowned in the Columbia River having crossed the Rockies. Today there are over 100 species of tree, including a rare Hinoki cypress, one of the five sacred trees of Japan.

David Nash, pictured above, made this sculpture, Forms That Grow in the Night, for the Pinetum in 2009. He was inspired by the black hollow in a nearby tree.

PAXTON 80

THE 20th-CENTURY GARDEN

From top to bottom:

Rose Garden

Ravine

Cottage Garden

Sensory Garden

Serpentine Hedge

"Amanda and I walk around the garden most mornings. It gives us a chance to see what has happened in the garden and to consider new ideas, so these walks are quite busy. We often find ourselves having to get back to the house in a hurry when we hear the Stables clock chiming 8 o'clock."

The Duke of Devonshire

Today the garden is managed by a team of 18 gardeners and trainees. They work with the present Duke and Duchess to preserve its layers of history, diversify the botanical collection and develop new features for visitors. There is a long term plan to introduce new species each year, especially trees and shrubs, particularly in the Arboretum and Pinetum. Only a few years ago, some were considered too tender for the Derbyshire climate, such as the *Eucryphia* (right).

A long-overgrown area, 'Quebec', was re-established in 2008 (below).
This led to the rediscovery of a 300 year old cascade (opposite).

"The best bit about melons for me is sowing the seed and then waiting as the seedling starts to break the surface of the compost. This is where the process starts."

Stefan Homerski, Kitchen Garden Supervisor

The kitchen gardeners grow over 100 varieties of fruit, 246 varieties of flowers and 158 varieties of vegetables, including 19 different potatoes and 38 different herbs.

DINING   62

Chatsworth has grown its own food for centuries. Bess of Hardwick built the first kitchen garden in the 1500s. The 11th Duke and Duchess created this one in 1991-94. Amongst the plants that can be found here are 'mummy peas', thought to have grown from peas discovered in Tutankhamun's tomb in 1922.

...e has three
... and
...a *amazonica*
...anana.
...rth in the
...make this
...e are two of
...Chatsworth
...**Vall** and the
...pricots grow
...Wall. Whilst
...grapes and
...d collection.
...nts and
...roughout
...**ouse**, which
...s as are the
...ctions from
where you can view the tropical section.

Conservative Wall (top).

Vinery (middle).

Service House (bottom).

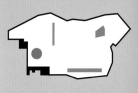

Sculpture has been a part of the landscape for 300 years. The present Duke and Duchess and the Chatsworth House Trust commission new sculptures to add to the collection that has grown since the 1st Duke's time.

Déjeuner sur l'Herbe, by Allen Jones, pictured with the Duke (right), in Quebec.

Pan, one of the 1st Duke's sculptures, by the Willow Tree Fountain.

Figure of a Man, by William Turnbull, at the edge of the Pinetum.

Moon Bean, by Simon Thomas, at the north end of the Arboretum.

Cornwall Slate Line, by Richard Long, beside the Canal Pond.

Walking Madonna, by
Dame Elisabeth Frink.

Lying Down Horse, by
Dame Elisabeth Frink,
north of the Grotto Pond.

Drummer, by Barry
Flanagan, by the Grotto
Pond.

The sculptures on the
Broad Walk were
cleaned in 2009.

*"Much thought is put into the
positioning of each new piece of
sculpture in the garden, often
prompting heated debate
amongst us all. This just goes to
show how much sculpture is an
integral element of the garden."*

The Duchess of Devonshire

"All the restaurants and events rooms at the Stables have undergone a transformation. This was a chance for me to decorate an area to make visitors feel comfortable and relaxed."

The Duchess of Devonshire

The 4th Duke hired the architect James Paine to build the Stables in the 1760s.

It was unusually richly decorated for the time, and was as much a decorative feature of his new park as a functional necessity. It had stalls for 80 horses and staff accommodation on the floors above. Paine was influenced by William Kent's 1732 design for the Royal Mews at Charing Cross, which were later demolished. Today the Stables contain restaurants and shops. Members of staff still work and live on the first floor.

One of a series of paintings of Chatsworth by Kitty North in the Carriage House Restaurant (below).
Grooms in the early 20th century (bottom).
Horses occupied the Stables until 1939 (below left).

WELCOME TO THE FARMYARD AND ADVENTURE PLAYGROUND

A member of the team will be happy to tell you about the daily choice of family activities.

Adventure Playground

Poultry

Milking demonstration

Cattle and sheep

Fish

Oak Barn

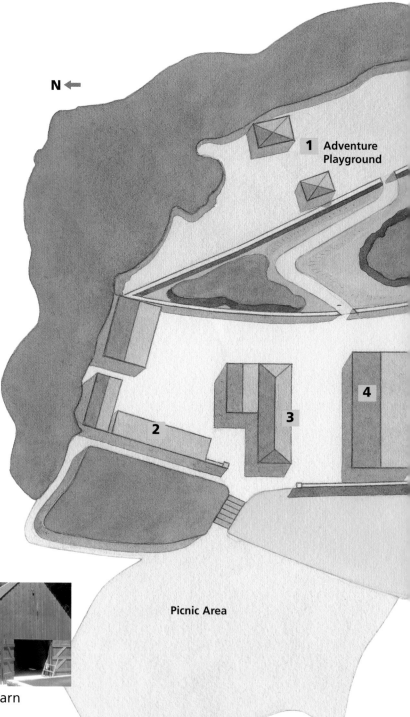

N ←

1 Adventure Playground

Picnic Area

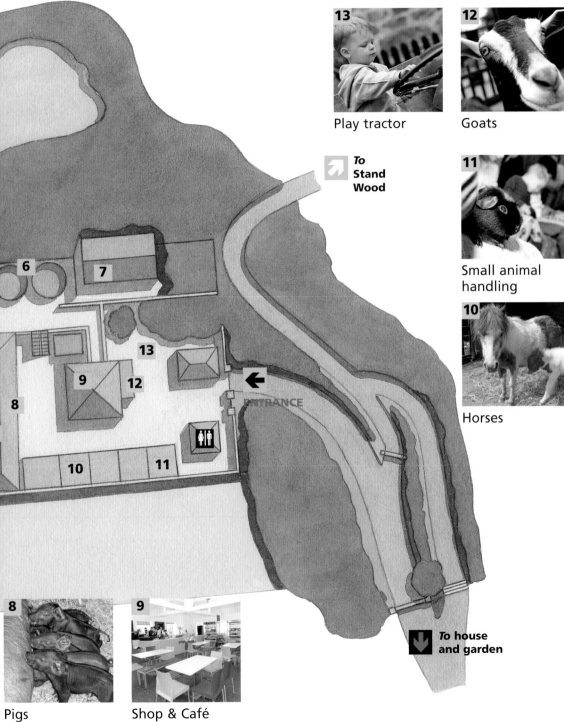

13
Play tractor

12
Goats

To **Stand Wood**

11
Small animal handling

10
Horses

8
Pigs

9
Shop & Café

To **house and garden**

"We are always planning new ideas for family fun, from milking demonstrations and animal handling sessions to hands-on farming days and Christmas nativities complete with farm animals."

Margaret Norris, Farmyard Manager

The Farmyard opened in 1973 to show how we use the land around Chatsworth to produce food and other materials.

Today visitors can learn how the animals are cared for, watch milking demonstrations, take part in animal handling sessions, enjoy trailer rides in the park and surrounding woodland and even book a day helping the farmyard team with their daily tasks. The Farmyard operates a carefully planned breeding programme so that there are young animals to see throughout most of the year. There is also a growing range of seasonal events and activities for all the family.

The building yard (top) before it was transformed into the milking parlour (above).
The Adventure Playground was opened in 1984, replaced in 1998 and a new climbing forest was added in 2012 (bottom).

WELCOME TO
STAND WOOD

Stand Wood is open to walkers throughout the year. There are many paths for you to explore. Here are a couple that we recommend.

○ ○ ○ ○ ○
EASY GOING TRAIL
Terrain: Road
Distance: 3.5 miles
Time: Allow 2 hours

○ ○ ○ ○ ○
EXPLORER'S WALK
Terrain: Steep in places with steps
Distance: 1 mile
Time: Allow 45 minutes

NOTES
• Woodland paths can be damp and slippery. Stout shoes or walking boots are best.
• Look out for farm traffic on tracks and tarmac drives.

Emperor Stream

Brownhill Oak

Dell

Emperor Lake

Hunting Tower

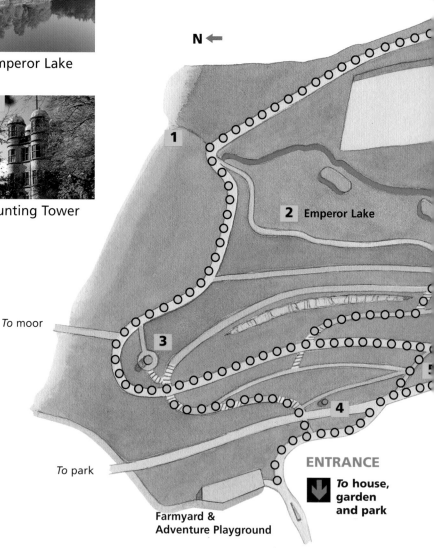

N ←

1

2 Emperor Lake

To moor

3

To park

4

ENTRANCE
To house, garden and park

Farmyard & Adventure Playground

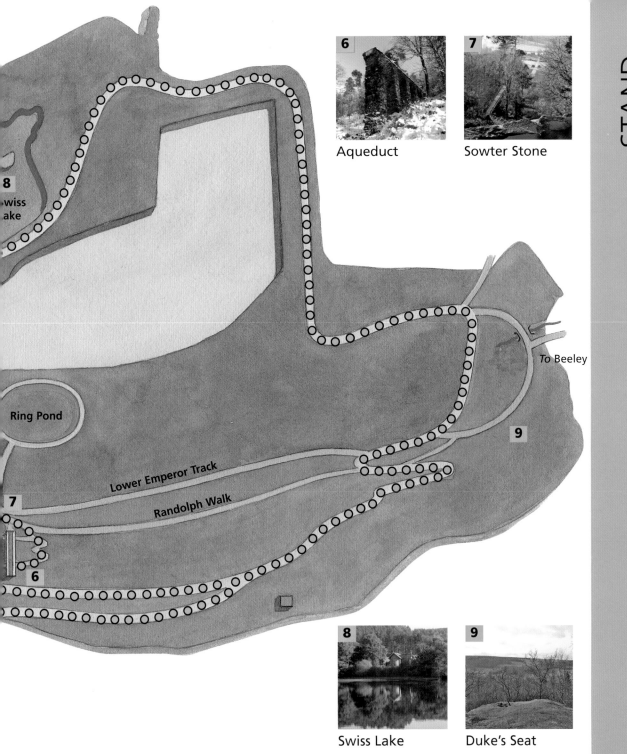

Aqueduct

Sowter Stone

Swiss Lake

Duke's Seat

To Beeley

Ring Pond

Lower Emperor Track

Randolph Walk

"I felt it extremely important that the holiday cottage interiors should carefully reflect the architecture and heritage of each building; the Hunting Tower (above) with its gothic references, and Swiss Cottage, named as such by the 6th Duke, thanks to his enthusiasm for all things Swiss."

The Duchess of Devonshire

The 4th Duke of Devonshire and his landscape gardener, 'Capability' Brown, enhanced and extended Stand Wood on a bare hillside in the 1760s. Some of the oldest trees are believed to be over 500 years old, and formed the western edge of the ancient Sherwood Forest. It was designed as a backdrop to the house and an extension of the pleasure grounds. The wood takes its name from the Stand, the hunting tower built by Bess of Hardwick in 1582 as a vantage point to watch the hunt in her deer park. The cannon outside the tower are from a ship that fought at Trafalgar in 1805. There are three man-made lakes in the wood which feed electricity turbines and water features in the garden and house. Joseph Paxton created the Emperor Stream and Emperor Lake in 1843 to feed the Emperor Fountain. He also enhanced the dramatic rock formations, built the 'ruined' Aqueduct below the Sowter Stone, laid out paths, steps and a scenic carriage route and built the ornamental Swiss Cottage. Today, both this and the Hunting Tower are holiday cottages.

Emperor Lake (top).
View from the Hunting Tower (bottom).

"Creating the new Warren woodland is the largest tree-planting project at Chatsworth for over 90 years. We are gradually planting over 38,000 trees and shrubs."

Roy Lingard, Head Forester

Today around a tenth of the estate, 1500 hectares, is woodland. Over the centuries, different generations have planted trees for different reasons, including timber production, hunting and landscaping. One of the priorities has always been to create continuous tree cover on the skyline, particularly around the house. Chatsworth's foresters work with the Forestry Commission to agree a sustainable management plan. They are also gradually planting 40 hectares of native woodland to the south of Stand Wood in an area once used to rear rabbits known as 'The Warren'.

The Warren in 2009 (top), and an impression of how it will look in 100 years' time (bottom).

THE ESTATE OFFICE

The estate's land-based
businesses are run by
a land agent from the
Estate Office, opposite
Edensor village.

A surveyor maintains
accurate maps of the
estate and a buildings
contracts manager
manages the upkeep of
over 400 houses and farm
buildings. The accounts,
human resources and
trading departments are
also based here.

QUARRIES

Chatsworth house was
built from local millstone
grit and is still repaired
using stone from the
original quarries. Various
companies operate
quarries on the estate.
Some produce over
300,000 tonnes of
limestone a year, others
specialise in masonry
stone.

WOODLAND

The foresters maintain the
woodland which makes
up a tenth of the estate,
mainly at Chatsworth and
Scarcliffe to the east.
Some trees are harvested
for building materials,
and the survival of
woodland is an essential
part of the stewardship
of the estate.

FISHING

The Chatsworth Fishery
occupies the stretch of the
River Derwent in the park
between Baslow and
Rowsley. A river keeper
maintains the banks and
weirs, and the fishing club
offers some of the finest
fly-fishing in Derbyshire.

MOORLAND

Members of the game department preserve important moorland habitats, manage miles of permissive footpaths on the moor and maintain the pheasant shoot. They control vermin which destroy young birds, lambs and trees.

INDUSTRY

The Chatsworth estate has been a site for clay production and lead, coal and iron ore mining. The Staveley Works on the estate near Chesterfield has seen iron, steel and chemical production since its creation in the 1780s.

TOURISM

Chatsworth has welcomed visitors for centuries and today tourism on the estate is an industry in itself. A variety of shops, pubs, restaurants and hotels, large and small, are managed by the estate and its tenants.

THE CHATSWORTH ESTATE COVERS AROUND 14,000 HECTARES OF DERBYSHIRE AND STAFFORDSHIRE.

Archaeological features in the landscape show that people have farmed the land around Chatsworth for thousands of years.

TENANTS

There are more than 100 farms and other enterprises on the estate operated by tenants.

BEEF

Dunsa Farm near Edensor supports a beef herd of 100 pedigree Limousin and 100 part-bred Limousin suckler cows.

DEER

There are two types of deer in the park, a herd of fallow deer and a herd of red deer. The smaller fallow deer has a white and brown coat. The red deer (above) with its reddish-brown coat is Britain's largest native mammal.

SHEEP

Chatsworth's shepherds look after more than 2,000 sheep that graze the grassland and moorland around the house. Most are Mule (cross breed) ewes, with around 650 Swaledales and 50 Jacobs, a breed that has been at Chatsworth for at least 250 years.

ARABLE

Wheat, barley, potatoes, oil seed rape, linseed and peas are grown on the estate's 400 hectare Elm Tree Farm, around 20 miles to the east of Chatsworth house. Some of the potatoes are sold at the Farm Shop, others are sold to Walkers to make crisps.

BREWERY

Beer was brewed at the Chatsworth Stables from the 1760s, and was part of staff wages until 1931. In 2005 the Peak Ales microbrewery opened on the estate. Evidence of gardeners tapping into the pipe which supplied beer to the House has inspired one of its beers, made to an original recipe, Gardener's Tap.

FARM SHOP

Much of the food produced on the estate is sold at the Farm Shop at Pilsley. Since 1977 it has sourced a wide variety of food from the closest possible suppliers.

A passion for environmental concerns is not new at Chatsworth. Sustainability and the environment have been important since the early 1800s. The 6th Duke developed the sustainable water features in the garden, using water from the nearby lakes. In the late 1800s, Chatsworth's first water powered turbine was installed to provide electricity in the house. Lord Burlington, son of the 12th Duke and Duchess, set up the Devonshire Group Environmental Committee to promote environmental awareness across the estate. In January 2011 we announced our vision to ensure Chatsworth's on-going commitment to sustainability. To find out more please visit our website at www.chatsworth.org/green

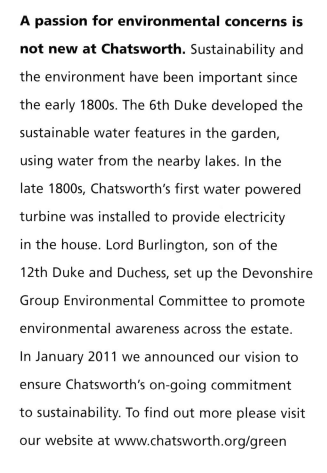

We're feeling a little green
The water used to flush these toilets is supplied from the lakes above the house. It is not perfectly clear but it is clean.

"We want to develop, steer and promote an evolving policy of environmental awareness and social responsibility with a vision to ensure Chatsworth's on-going commitment to sustainability with the philosophy 'reduce, reuse, recycle' at its heart."

Lord Burlington

Green Tourism
SILVER

The Chatsworth estate is a journey of discovery for educational groups.

The house provides a depth of study for all students. Art, history, social studies, archaeology, leisure and tourism are all subjects that can be explored alongside one of our engaging and enthusiastic guides. The 105 acre garden as well as being beautiful has a rich source of educational material to discover, from the power behind the waterworks to the modern sculpture exhibitions. The farmyard provides both outdoor educational tours and indoor activity sessions including subjects such as animal care. There are also extremely popular tractor and trailer rides around Stand Wood, where students can learn about the flora and fauna and the work of the forestry, game and farms departments. For more information please visit our website at www.chatsworth.org/schools or call 01246 565430.

"I live in Park Cottage (right), the only house that remained in the park after the 4th Duke began to move Edensor village in the 1760s."

Rob Dowding, Garden Supervisor

The main estate surrounding the house includes the park and the villages of Pilsley, Edensor (pronounced 'Enza'), Beeley and Calton Lees. Many of Chatsworth's several hundred employees and pensioners live here.

The 6th Duke and Joseph Paxton rebuilt Edensor village, combining a variety of architectural styles (opposite).

Pupils from the local school, Pilsley Church of England Primary, visiting Chatsworth garden (left).

Calton Lees (top).

Pilsley (above).

A team of curators, archivists, textile conservators and a photo librarian care for the objects in the collection and help people to study them.

BUILDING SERVICES

An in-house team of skilled builders, joiners, plumbers and electricians cares for the house. Beneath its half a hectare lead roof there are over 300 rooms, 17 staircases, 459 windows and 2,084 light bulbs.

WELCOMING VISITORS

In the 1700s, the Head Housekeeper was allowed to show visitors around the house. In the 21st century, Chatsworth, open from March through to December, continues to welcome more visitors than ever. The house is beautifully styled in November and December for Christmas with a new theme each year.

LANDSCAPE MANAGEMENT

The landscape needs constant management by gardeners, foresters, **domain** workers, gamekeepers and river keepers. Modern equipment means that these teams are smaller today, but historic skills such as dry stone walling still survive.

FOOD AND FARMING

The land around Chatsworth is farmed by stockmen, shepherds and tenant farmers. They supply food to the Farm Shop at Pilsley, which employs butchers, bakers and fishmongers. The estate traditionally brewed its own beer. Today it is produced on the estate at the Peak Ales brewery.

ESTATE MANAGEMENT

Bess of Hardwick initialled every page of her account books. Today this painstaking accounting continues at the Estate Office, with all the benefits of complex computer programs.

CHATSWORTH IS A WORKING COMMUNITY, WHERE OLD SKILLS SURVIVE ALONGSIDE NEW TECHNOLOGIES.

GLOSSARY

Balustrade
A row of repeating small posts, or 'balusters', that support a rail.

Baroque
Relating to a theatrical style in art and architecture that emphasised dramatic forms, irregular shapes and extravagant decoration and which flourished in Europe from the early 1600s to the mid-1700s.

Bas-relief
Sculpture in which the forms project slightly from a flat background but no part is completely detached from it.

Belvedere
An open, roofed structure which commands a wide view.

Classical
Relating to the ancient Greeks and Romans and their ideals of order and harmony, especially in art, architecture and literature.

Colonnade
A structure composed of columns placed at regular intervals.

Delftware
Glazed earthenware pottery, usually blue and white, made at the city of Delft in Holland.

Domain
The domain department cares for the park, its trees, lakes, conduits, paths and boundaries.

Enfilade
A series of doors that provide a view through a suite of rooms when open.

Glorious Revolution
The events of 1688 in England that resulted in the overthrow of King James II and the crowning of William III (William of Orange) and Mary II as joint monarchs.

Grand Tour
An extended tour of continental Europe combining education and pleasure, undertaken by many young men of the English upper class between the late 1600s and early 1800s.

Incunabula
Books printed before 1501, in the cradle days of printing. The word derives from the Latin for 'cradle'.

Old Master
A distinguished European artist, especially a painter, working between about 1500 and the early 1700s, or a work created by one of these artists.

Palladian
Relating to an architectural style of the mid-1700s derived from that of Andrea Palladio, characterised by classical forms and arched openings.

Renaissance
A revival of classical art, architecture, literature and learning that began in Italy in the 1400s and later spread throughout Europe.

Whig
A member of a British political party in the 1700s and 1800s which championed liberal reform.

For more information, including a suggested reading list, visit
www.chatsworth.org

Chatsworth House Trust,
Bakewell, Derbyshire, DE45 1PP
Tel: 01246 565300
Email: visit@chatsworth.org

DESIGN
Peter Drew / Phrogg Design
07926 882000

TEXT
Claire Fowler

IMAGES
Diane Naylor

PROJECT MANAGEMENT
Heather Redmond, Debbie Wayment

PHOTOGRAPHY
June Buck, Matthew Bullen, Bill Burlington, David Dawson, Peter Drew, The Duchess of Devonshire, Jude Gadd, Brian Gilbert, Diane Naylor, Peter Packer, Gary Rogers, David Vintiner.

LIBRARY PHOTOGRAPHY
Bernard Cox/Stapleton Collection/Bridgeman Art Library, Bibliothèque Nationale Paris, Burghley House Collection, Devonshire Collection, 'Louis Laguerre' reproduced with kind permission of His Grace the Duke of Marlborough, 'William III' image courtesy of Mealy's Images, National Portrait Gallery, National Trust, Norman Parkinson Archive, PDNPA, Reunion des Musée Nationaux, Royal Collection © 2010 Her Majesty Queen Elizabeth II.

For full image credits please visit www.chatsworth.org

ILLUSTRATIONS
Robert Calow

Printed by Greenshires.

With thanks to everybody at Chatsworth who has assisted in the production of this book.

ISBN 978-0-953732-91-3

First published by Chatsworth House Trust 2010. Revised editions 2011, 2012, 2013.